"Always carry a flagon of whiskey in case of
snakebite and furthermore
always carry a small snake."

W.C. Fields

Published by: WTW Books
©2018 WTW Books

Date:

NAME: ....

TYPE: ....

AGE: ....

AROMA: ....

TASTE: --

RATING: 1   2   3   4   5   6   7   8   9   10

NOTES:

Date:

NAME: ....

TYPE: ....

AGE: ....

AROMA: ....

TASTE: ---

RATING: 1   2   3   4   5   6   7   8   9   10

NOTES:

Date:

NAME: ....

TYPE: ....

AGE: ....

AROMA: ....

TASTE: ---

RATING: 1   2   3   4   5   6   7   8   9   10

NOTES:

Date:

NAME: ....

TYPE: ....

AGE: ....

AROMA: ....

TASTE: --

RATING: 1   2   3   4   5   6   7   8   9   10

NOTES:

Date:

NAME: ....

TYPE: ....

AGE: ....

AROMA: ....

TASTE: --

RATING: 1   2   3   4   5   6   7   8   9   10

NOTES:

Date:

NAME: ....

TYPE: ....

AGE: ....

AROMA: ....

TASTE: --

RATING: 1   2   3   4   5   6   7   8   9   10

NOTES:

Date:

NAME: ....

TYPE: ....

AGE: ....

AROMA: ....

TASTE: --

RATING: 1   2   3   4   5   6   7   8   9   10

NOTES:

Date:

NAME: ....

TYPE: ....

AGE: ....

AROMA: ....

TASTE: --

RATING: 1   2   3   4   5   6   7   8   9   10

NOTES:

Date:

NAME: ....

TYPE: ....

AGE: ....

AROMA: ....

TASTE: --

RATING: 1   2   3   4   5   6   7   8   9   10

NOTES:

Date:

NAME: ....

TYPE: ....

AGE: ....

AROMA: ....

TASTE: ....

RATING:　　　1　2　3　4　5　6　7　8　9　10

NOTES:

Date:

NAME:

TYPE:

AGE:

AROMA:

TASTE:

RATING:　　　1　2　3　4　5　6　7　8　9　10

NOTES:

Date:

NAME: ....

TYPE: ....

AGE: ....

AROMA: ....

TASTE: --

RATING:　　　1　2　3　4　5　6　7　8　9　10

NOTES:

Date:

NAME: ....

TYPE: ....

AGE: ....

AROMA: ....

TASTE: --

RATING: 1   2   3   4   5   6   7   8   9   10

NOTES:

Date:

NAME: ....

TYPE: ....

AGE: ....

AROMA: ....

TASTE: --

RATING: 1   2   3   4   5   6   7   8   9   10

NOTES:

Date:

NAME:

....

TYPE:

....

AGE:

....

AROMA:

....

TASTE:

- -

RATING: 1 2 3 4 5 6 7 8 9 10

NOTES:

- -

- -

- -

- -

- -

- -

Date:

NAME: ....

TYPE: ....

AGE: ....

AROMA: ....

TASTE: ---

RATING: 1   2   3   4   5   6   7   8   9   10

NOTES:

Date:

NAME: ....

TYPE: ....

AGE: ....

AROMA: ....

TASTE: --

RATING: 1   2   3   4   5   6   7   8   9   10

NOTES:

Date:

NAME: ....

TYPE: ....

AGE: ....

AROMA: ....

TASTE: --

RATING: 1   2   3   4   5   6   7   8   9   10

NOTES:

Date:

NAME: ....

TYPE: ....

AGE: ....

AROMA: ....

TASTE: --

RATING: 1   2   3   4   5   6   7   8   9   10

NOTES:

Date:

NAME: ....

TYPE: ....

AGE: ....

AROMA: ....

TASTE: --

RATING: 1   2   3   4   5   6   7   8   9   10

NOTES:

Date:

NAME: ....

TYPE: ....

AGE: ....

AROMA: ....

TASTE: --

RATING: 1   2   3   4   5   6   7   8   9   10

NOTES:

Date:

NAME: ....

TYPE: ....

AGE: ....

AROMA: ....

TASTE: --

RATING: 1   2   3   4   5   6   7   8   9   10

NOTES:

Date:

NAME: ....

TYPE: ....

AGE: ....

AROMA: ....

TASTE: ....

RATING: 1   2   3   4   5   6   7   8   9   10

NOTES:

Date:

NAME: ....

TYPE: ....

AGE: ....

AROMA: ....

TASTE: ---

RATING: 1 2 3 4 5 6 7 8 9 10

NOTES:

Date:

NAME: ....

TYPE: ....

AGE: ....

AROMA: ....

TASTE: --

RATING: 1   2   3   4   5   6   7   8   9   10

NOTES:

Date:

NAME: ....

TYPE: ....

AGE: ....

AROMA: ....

TASTE: --

RATING: 1   2   3   4   5   6   7   8   9   10

NOTES:

Date:

NAME: ....

TYPE: ....

AGE: ....

AROMA: ....

TASTE: -

RATING: 1   2   3   4   5   6   7   8   9   10

NOTES:

- -

- -

- -

- -

- -

- -

Date:

NAME: ....

TYPE: ....

AGE: ....

AROMA: ....

TASTE: ---

RATING: 1   2   3   4   5   6   7   8   9   10

NOTES:

Date:

NAME: ....

TYPE: ....

AGE: ....

AROMA: ....

TASTE: ....

RATING: 1   2   3   4   5   6   7   8   9   10

NOTES:

....

....

....

....

....

....

Date:

NAME: ....

TYPE: ....

AGE: ....

AROMA: ....

TASTE: --

RATING: 1   2   3   4   5   6   7   8   9   10

NOTES:

Date:

NAME: ....

TYPE: ....

AGE: ....

AROMA: ....

TASTE: ---

RATING: 1   2   3   4   5   6   7   8   9   10

NOTES:

Date:

NAME: ....

TYPE: ....

AGE: ....

AROMA: ....

TASTE: --

RATING: 1   2   3   4   5   6   7   8   9   10

NOTES:

Date:

NAME: ....

TYPE: ....

AGE: ....

AROMA: ....

TASTE: ---

RATING: 1   2   3   4   5   6   7   8   9   10

NOTES:

Date:

NAME: ....

TYPE: ....

AGE: ....

AROMA: ....

TASTE: --

RATING: 1   2   3   4   5   6   7   8   9   10

NOTES:

Date:

NAME: ....

TYPE: ....

AGE: ....

AROMA: ....

TASTE: --

RATING: 1   2   3   4   5   6   7   8   9   10

NOTES:

Date:

NAME: ....

TYPE: ....

AGE: ....

AROMA: ....

TASTE: --

RATING: 1   2   3   4   5   6   7   8   9   10

NOTES:

Date:

NAME: ....

TYPE: ....

AGE: ....

AROMA: ....

TASTE: ---

RATING: 1   2   3   4   5   6   7   8   9   10

NOTES:

Date:

NAME: ....

TYPE: ....

AGE: ....

AROMA: ....

TASTE: --

RATING: 1   2   3   4   5   6   7   8   9   10

NOTES:

Date:

NAME: ....

TYPE: ....

AGE: ....

AROMA: ....

TASTE: --

RATING: 1 2 3 4 5 6 7 8 9 10

NOTES:

Date:

NAME: ....

TYPE: ....

AGE: ....

AROMA: ....

TASTE: --

RATING: 1   2   3   4   5   6   7   8   9   10

NOTES:

Date:

NAME: ....

TYPE: ....

AGE: ....

AROMA: ....

TASTE: --

RATING: 1   2   3   4   5   6   7   8   9   10

NOTES:

Date:

NAME: ....

TYPE: ....

AGE: ....

AROMA: ....

TASTE: ---

RATING: 1   2   3   4   5   6   7   8   9   10

NOTES:

Date:

NAME: ....

TYPE: ....

AGE: ....

AROMA: ....

TASTE: --

RATING: 1   2   3   4   5   6   7   8   9   10

NOTES:

Date:

NAME: ....

TYPE: ....

AGE: ....

AROMA: ....

TASTE: --

RATING: 1   2   3   4   5   6   7   8   9   10

NOTES:

Date:

NAME: ....

TYPE: ....

AGE: ....

AROMA: ....

TASTE: --

RATING: 1   2   3   4   5   6   7   8   9   10

NOTES:

Date:

NAME: ....

TYPE: ....

AGE: ....

AROMA: ....

TASTE: --

RATING: 1   2   3   4   5   6   7   8   9   10

NOTES:

Date:

NAME: ....

TYPE: ....

AGE: ....

AROMA: ....

TASTE: --

RATING: 1 2 3 4 5 6 7 8 9 10

NOTES:

Date:

NAME: ....

TYPE: ....

AGE: ....

AROMA: ....

TASTE: --

RATING: 1   2   3   4   5   6   7   8   9   10

NOTES:

Date:

NAME: ....

TYPE: ....

AGE: ....

AROMA: ....

TASTE: ....

RATING: 1 2 3 4 5 6 7 8 9 10

NOTES:

Date:

NAME: ....

TYPE: ....

AGE: ....

AROMA: ....

TASTE: --

RATING: 1   2   3   4   5   6   7   8   9   10

NOTES:

Date:

NAME: ....

TYPE: ....

AGE: ....

AROMA: ....

TASTE: --

RATING:　　　1　2　3　4　5　6　7　8　9　10

NOTES:

Date:

NAME: ....

TYPE: ....

AGE: ....

AROMA: ....

TASTE: ---

RATING: 1   2   3   4   5   6   7   8   9   10

NOTES:

Date:

NAME: ....

TYPE: ....

AGE: ....

AROMA: ....

TASTE: --

RATING: 1 2 3 4 5 6 7 8 9 10

NOTES:

Date:

NAME: ....

TYPE: ....

AGE: ....

AROMA: ....

TASTE: --

RATING: 1   2   3   4   5   6   7   8   9   10

NOTES:

Date:

NAME: ....

TYPE: ....

AGE: ....

AROMA: ....

TASTE: ....

RATING: 1   2   3   4   5   6   7   8   9   10

NOTES:

....

....

....

....

....

....

....

Date:

NAME: ....

TYPE: ....

AGE: ....

AROMA: ....

TASTE: ....

RATING: 1   2   3   4   5   6   7   8   9   10

NOTES:

....

....

....

....

....

....

Date:

NAME: ....

TYPE: ....

AGE: ....

AROMA: ....

TASTE: --

RATING: 1   2   3   4   5   6   7   8   9   10

NOTES:

Date:

NAME: ....

TYPE: ....

AGE: ....

AROMA: ....

TASTE: --

RATING: 1 2 3 4 5 6 7 8 9 10

NOTES:

Date:

NAME: ....

TYPE: ....

AGE: ....

AROMA: ....

TASTE: ....

RATING: 1   2   3   4   5   6   7   8   9   10

NOTES:

Date:

NAME: ....

TYPE: ....

AGE: ....

AROMA: ....

TASTE: ---

RATING: 1   2   3   4   5   6   7   8   9   10

NOTES:

Date:

NAME: ....

TYPE: ....

AGE: ....

AROMA: ....

TASTE: ---

RATING: 1   2   3   4   5   6   7   8   9   10

NOTES:

Date:

NAME: ....

TYPE: ....

AGE: ....

AROMA: ....

TASTE: ---

RATING: 1   2   3   4   5   6   7   8   9   10

NOTES:

Date:

NAME: ....

TYPE: ....

AGE: ....

AROMA: ....

TASTE: --

RATING: 1 2 3 4 5 6 7 8 9 10

NOTES:

Date:

NAME: ....

TYPE: ....

AGE: ....

AROMA: ....

TASTE: ---

RATING: 1   2   3   4   5   6   7   8   9   10

NOTES:

Date:

NAME: ....

TYPE: ....

AGE: ....

AROMA: ....

TASTE: --

RATING: 1   2   3   4   5   6   7   8   9   10

NOTES:

Date:

NAME: ....

TYPE: ....

AGE: ....

AROMA: ....

TASTE: ---

RATING: 1 2 3 4 5 6 7 8 9 10

NOTES:

Date:

NAME: ....

TYPE: ....

AGE: ....

AROMA: ....

TASTE: --

RATING: 1 2 3 4 5 6 7 8 9 10

NOTES:

Date:

NAME: ....

TYPE: ....

AGE: ....

AROMA: ....

TASTE: --

RATING: 1   2   3   4   5   6   7   8   9   10

NOTES:

Date:

NAME: ....

TYPE: ....

AGE: ....

AROMA: ....

TASTE: --

RATING: 1   2   3   4   5   6   7   8   9   10

NOTES:

Date:

NAME: ....

TYPE: ....

AGE: ....

AROMA: ....

TASTE: --

RATING: 1 2 3 4 5 6 7 8 9 10

NOTES:

Date:

NAME: ....

TYPE: ....

AGE: ....

AROMA: ....

TASTE: ....

RATING: 1 2 3 4 5 6 7 8 9 10

NOTES:

Date:

NAME: ....

TYPE: ....

AGE: ....

AROMA: ....

TASTE: ---

RATING: 1   2   3   4   5   6   7   8   9   10

NOTES:

Date:

NAME: ....

TYPE: ....

AGE: ....

AROMA: ....

TASTE: ....

RATING: 1   2   3   4   5   6   7   8   9   10

NOTES:

Date:

NAME: ....

TYPE: ....

AGE: ....

AROMA: ....

TASTE: ....

RATING: 1   2   3   4   5   6   7   8   9   10

NOTES:

....

....

....

....

....

....

Date:

NAME: ....

TYPE: ....

AGE: ....

AROMA: ....

TASTE: -

RATING: 1 2 3 4 5 6 7 8 9 10

NOTES:

Date:

NAME: ....

TYPE: ....

AGE: ....

AROMA: ....

TASTE: ---

RATING: 1 2 3 4 5 6 7 8 9 10

NOTES:

Date:

NAME: ....

TYPE: ....

AGE: ....

AROMA: ....

TASTE: ....

RATING: 1 2 3 4 5 6 7 8 9 10

NOTES:

....

....

....

....

....

....

Date:

NAME: ....

TYPE: ....

AGE: ....

AROMA: ....

TASTE: --

RATING: 1 2 3 4 5 6 7 8 9 10

NOTES:

Date:

NAME: ....

TYPE: ....

AGE: ....

AROMA: ....

TASTE: --

RATING: 1 2 3 4 5 6 7 8 9 10

NOTES:

Date:

NAME: ....

TYPE: ....

AGE: ....

AROMA: ....

TASTE: --

RATING: 1   2   3   4   5   6   7   8   9   10

NOTES:

Date:

NAME: ....

TYPE: ....

AGE: ....

AROMA: ....

TASTE: --

RATING: 1   2   3   4   5   6   7   8   9   10

NOTES:

Date:

NAME: ....

TYPE: ....

AGE: ....

AROMA: ....

TASTE: ....

RATING: 1   2   3   4   5   6   7   8   9   10

NOTES:

....

....

....

....

....

....

Date:

NAME: ....

TYPE: ....

AGE: ....

AROMA: ....

TASTE: _____

RATING: 1 2 3 4 5 6 7 8 9 10

NOTES:

_____

_____

_____

_____

_____

_____

Date:

NAME: ....

TYPE: ....

AGE: ....

AROMA: ....

TASTE: ....

RATING: 1   2   3   4   5   6   7   8   9   10

NOTES:

....

....

....

....

....

....

Date:

NAME: ....

TYPE: ....

AGE: ....

AROMA: ....

TASTE: --

RATING: 1   2   3   4   5   6   7   8   9   10

NOTES:

Date:

NAME: ....

TYPE: ....

AGE: ....

AROMA: ....

TASTE: --

RATING: 1 2 3 4 5 6 7 8 9 10

NOTES:

Date:

NAME: ....

TYPE: ....

AGE: ....

AROMA: ....

TASTE: --

RATING: 1   2   3   4   5   6   7   8   9   10

NOTES:

Date:

NAME: ....

TYPE: ....

AGE: ....

AROMA: ....

TASTE: --

RATING: 1 2 3 4 5 6 7 8 9 10

NOTES:

Date:

NAME: ....

TYPE: ....

AGE: ....

AROMA: ....

TASTE: --

RATING: 1   2   3   4   5   6   7   8   9   10

NOTES:

Date:

NAME: ....

TYPE: ....

AGE: ....

AROMA: ....

TASTE: --

RATING: 1   2   3   4   5   6   7   8   9   10

NOTES:

Date:

NAME: ....

TYPE: ....

AGE: ....

AROMA: ....

TASTE: --

RATING: 1   2   3   4   5   6   7   8   9   10

NOTES:

Date:

NAME: ....

TYPE: ....

AGE: ....

AROMA: ....

TASTE: ....

RATING: 1   2   3   4   5   6   7   8   9   10

NOTES:

Date:

NAME: ....

TYPE: ....

AGE: ....

AROMA: ....

TASTE: ....

RATING: 1 2 3 4 5 6 7 8 9 10

NOTES:

....

....

....

....

....

....

Date:

NAME: ....

TYPE: ....

AGE: ....

AROMA: ....

TASTE: --

RATING: 1   2   3   4   5   6   7   8   9   10

NOTES:

Date:

NAME: ....

TYPE: ....

AGE: ....

AROMA: ....

TASTE: --

RATING: 1   2   3   4   5   6   7   8   9   10

NOTES:

Date:

NAME: ....

TYPE: ....

AGE: ....

AROMA: ....

TASTE: --

RATING: 1   2   3   4   5   6   7   8   9   10

NOTES:

Date:

NAME: ....

TYPE: ....

AGE: ....

AROMA: ....

TASTE: ---

RATING: 1   2   3   4   5   6   7   8   9   10

NOTES:

Date:

NAME: ....

TYPE: ....

AGE: ....

AROMA: ....

TASTE: ....

RATING: 1   2   3   4   5   6   7   8   9   10

NOTES:

....

....

....

....

....

Date:

NAME: ....

TYPE: ....

AGE: ....

AROMA: ....

TASTE: ---

RATING: 1   2   3   4   5   6   7   8   9   10

NOTES:

Date:

NAME: ....

TYPE: ....

AGE: ....

AROMA: ....

TASTE: ---

RATING: 1   2   3   4   5   6   7   8   9   10

NOTES:

Date:

NAME: ....

TYPE: ....

AGE: ....

AROMA: ....

TASTE: ---

RATING: 1 2 3 4 5 6 7 8 9 10

NOTES:

Date:

NAME: ....

TYPE: ....

AGE: ....

AROMA: ....

TASTE: --

RATING: 1   2   3   4   5   6   7   8   9   10

NOTES:

Date:

NAME: ....

TYPE: ....

AGE: ....

AROMA: ....

TASTE: ....

RATING: 1   2   3   4   5   6   7   8   9   10

NOTES:

....

....

....

....

....

....

....

Date:

NAME: ....

TYPE: ....

AGE: ....

AROMA: ....

TASTE: --

RATING: 1   2   3   4   5   6   7   8   9   10

NOTES:

Date:

NAME: ....

TYPE: ....

AGE: ....

AROMA: ....

TASTE: --

RATING: 1   2   3   4   5   6   7   8   9   10

NOTES:

Date:

NAME: ....

TYPE: ....

AGE: ....

AROMA: ....

TASTE: ....

RATING: 1   2   3   4   5   6   7   8   9   10

NOTES:

Date:

NAME: ....

TYPE: ....

AGE: ....

AROMA: ....

TASTE: --

RATING: 1 2 3 4 5 6 7 8 9 10

NOTES:

Date:

NAME: ....

TYPE: ....

AGE: ....

AROMA: ....

TASTE: --

RATING: 1   2   3   4   5   6   7   8   9   10

NOTES:

Date:

NAME: ....

TYPE: ....

AGE: ....

AROMA: ....

TASTE: --

RATING: 1   2   3   4   5   6   7   8   9   10

NOTES:

Date:

NAME: ....

TYPE: ....

AGE: ....

AROMA: ....

TASTE: --

RATING: 1   2   3   4   5   6   7   8   9   10

NOTES:

Date:

NAME: ....

TYPE: ....

AGE: ....

AROMA: ....

TASTE: ---

RATING: 1   2   3   4   5   6   7   8   9   10

NOTES:

Date:

NAME: ....

TYPE: ....

AGE: ....

AROMA: ....

TASTE: ....

RATING: 1   2   3   4   5   6   7   8   9   10

NOTES:

....

....

....

....

....

....

Date:

NAME: ....

TYPE: ....

AGE: ....

AROMA: ....

TASTE: --

RATING: 1   2   3   4   5   6   7   8   9   10

NOTES:

Date:

NAME: ....

TYPE: ....

AGE: ....

AROMA: ....

TASTE: ....

RATING: 1   2   3   4   5   6   7   8   9   10

NOTES:

_____

_____

_____

_____

_____

_____

Date:

NAME: ....

TYPE: ....

AGE: ....

AROMA: ....

TASTE: ....

RATING: 1 2 3 4 5 6 7 8 9 10

NOTES:

....

....

....

....

....

....

Date:

NAME: ....

TYPE: ....

AGE: ....

AROMA: ....

TASTE: --

RATING: 1   2   3   4   5   6   7   8   9   10

NOTES:

Date:

NAME: ....

TYPE: ....

AGE: ....

AROMA: ....

TASTE: --

RATING: 1   2   3   4   5   6   7   8   9   10

NOTES:

Date:

NAME: ....

TYPE: ....

AGE: ....

AROMA: ....

TASTE: ....

RATING: 1   2   3   4   5   6   7   8   9   10

NOTES:

....

....

....

....

....

....

Date:

NAME: ....

TYPE: ....

AGE: ....

AROMA: ....

TASTE: ....

RATING: 1   2   3   4   5   6   7   8   9   10

NOTES:

....

....

....

....

....

....

Date:

NAME:
....

TYPE:
....

AGE:
....

AROMA:
....

TASTE:

RATING: 1   2   3   4   5   6   7   8   9   10

NOTES:

Date:

NAME: ....

TYPE: ....

AGE: ....

AROMA: ....

TASTE: --

RATING: 1   2   3   4   5   6   7   8   9   10

NOTES:

Date:

NAME: ....

TYPE: ....

AGE: ....

AROMA: ....

TASTE: ....

RATING: 1 2 3 4 5 6 7 8 9 10

NOTES:

....

....

....

....

....

Date:

NAME: ....

TYPE: ....

AGE: ....

AROMA: ....

TASTE: --

RATING: 1   2   3   4   5   6   7   8   9   10

NOTES:

Date:

NAME: ....

TYPE: ....

AGE: ....

AROMA: ....

TASTE: _____

RATING: 1   2   3   4   5   6   7   8   9   10

NOTES:

_____

_____

_____

_____

_____

_____

Date:

NAME: ....

TYPE: ....

AGE: ....

AROMA: ....

TASTE: --

RATING: 1   2   3   4   5   6   7   8   9   10

NOTES:

Made in the USA
Monee, IL
30 September 2023

43756388R00080